D.I.Y. MAKE IT HAPPEN

YOUTUBE CHANNEL

VIRGINIA LOH-HAGAN

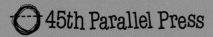45th Parallel Press

Published in the United States of America by Cherry Lake Publishing
Ann Arbor, Michigan
www.cherrylakepublishing.com

Reading Adviser: Marla Conn MS, Ed., Literacy specialist, Read-Ability, Inc.
Book Designer: Felicia Macheske

Photo Credits: © Julian Rovagnati/Shutterstock.com, cover, 1; © Billion Photos/Shutterstock.com, 3, 29; © Margot Petrowski/ Shutterstock.com, 5; © Monkey Business Images/Shutterstock.com, 9; © Norman Chan/Shutterstock.com, 10; © Claudia Paulussen/Shutterstock.com, 11; © szefei/Shutterstock.com, 12; © zhu difeng/Shutterstock.com; 14,30; © naluwan/ Shutterstock.com, 14; 31; © Namart Pieamsuwan/Shutterstock.com, 15; © nikitabuida/Shutterstock.com, 17; © Your Design / Shutterstock.com, 18; © George Rudy/Shutterstock.com, 20; © Lykovata/Shutterstock.com, 21, 31; © Julian Rovagnati/ Shutterstock.com, 22, 23; © Rob Marmion/Shutterstock.com, 25; © Nelosa/Shutterstock.com, 27; © wavebreakmedia/ Shutterstock.com, back cover;© Dora Zett/Shutterstock.com, back cover

Graphic Elements Throughout: © pashabo/Shutterstock.com; © axako/Shutterstock.com; © IreneArt/Shutterstock.com; © Katya Bogina/Shutterstock.com; © Belausava Volha/Shutterstock.com; © Nik Merkulov/Shutterstock.com; © Ya Tshey/ Shutterstock.com; © kubais/Shutterstock.com; © Sasha Nazim/Shutterstock.com; © Infomages/Shutterstock.com; © Ursa Major/Shutterstock.com; © topform/Shutterstock.com; © Art'nLera/Shutterstock.com;

45th Parallel Press is an imprint of Cherry Lake Publishing.

Library of Congress Cataloging-in-Publication Data

Names: Loh-Hagan, Virginia, author.
Title: YouTube Channel / by Virginia Loh-Hagan.
Other titles: You Tube Channel
Description: Ann Arbor : Cherry Lake Publishing, 2016. I Series: DIY projects
  I Includes bibliographical references and index.
Identifiers: LCCN 2016029717I ISBN 9781634721455 (hardcover) I ISBN
  9781634722117 (pdf) I ISBN 9781634722773 (pbk.) I ISBN 9781634723435 (ebook)
Subjects: LCSH: YouTube (Electronic resource)—Juvenile literature. I
  Internet videos—Juvenile literature.
Classification: LCC TK5105.8868.Y68 L64 2016 I DDC 006.7/5—dc23
LC record available at https://lccn.loc.gov/2016029717

Printed in the United States of America
Corporate Graphics

ABOUT THE AUTHOR

Dr. Virginia Loh-Hagan is an author, university professor, former classroom teacher, and curriculum designer. She likes watching YouTube channels. But she's more active on Facebook and Twitter. She lives in San Diego with her very tall husband and very naughty dogs. To learn more about her, visit www.virginialoh.com.

TABLE OF CONTENTS

CHAPTER ONE

WHAT DOES IT MEAN TO CREATE A YOUTUBE CHANNEL?

Do you love technology? Do you love filming? Do you love performing? Then, creating your own YouTube channel is the right project for you!

YouTube is a Web site. People post videos. People watch videos. **Users** love sharing videos. Users are people who use the Internet.

YouTube channels are profiles. Each channel organizes videos. Channels have owners. Owners create **content**. Content includes videos and comments. Owners control content. They design how channels look.

Watch YouTube channels. Learn from other owners.

KNOW THE LINGO

Avatar: image that represents a person

Bulletin: message sent to all subscribers

Embedding: code that is copied and pasted on Web pages so the video can be directly viewed

Favorites: list of favorite videos

Flag: to alert YouTube staff members that a video violates guidelines

Montage: video filled with images, or video clips set to music

Playlist: list of videos, way of organizing videos

RPM: "revenue per thousand" views, which is how people make money; a YouTube RPM can be anywhere between $2 and $15

Spam: advertising comments left by users

Trolls: people who leave mean comments

Video response: posting of a video in response to a video

Vlogs: video blogs, regularly updated video series

Watch time: actual amount of time people spend watching videos

Create a YouTube channel whenever you want! People watch online videos all the time.

Owners create channels for different reasons. They work on their skills. They share their work. They promote themselves. They build their **fan base**. Fan base means admirers.

YouTube owners have a community. They watch each other's videos. They comment. They review. They learn. They get inspired. They connect around a common interest.

You'll have fun making videos. You'll get better at your skills. You'll meet lots of people. The best part is sharing what you love.

Learn about online safety.

CHAPTER TWO

WHAT DO YOU NEED TO CREATE A YOUTUBE CHANNEL?

Get online tools.

➡ **Use a computer. Make sure it has lots of storage space. Storage holds data. It's the computer's memory. Videos need a lot of storage.**

➡ **Use the Internet. Make sure you have strong service.**

Get online **accounts**. Accounts give you Web site access. They're personal. Don't share passwords.

➡ **Get a Google mail address.**

- ➡ **Go to the YouTube site. Get an account.**

- ➡ **Enter a username. Enter a password.**

- ➡ **Click the button to create a channel.**

You need to be at least 13 years old to start your own official YouTube channel.

Get video equipment. You'll need to make videos. There are several options.

➡ **Use a smartphone. Smartphones have cameras. This is the most mobile option. Mobile means easy to move. You can take smartphones anywhere.**

➡ **Use a webcam. A webcam is a camera. It's on a computer. It's above the monitor.**

➡ **Use a video recording device. Transfer videos to computers.**

➡ **Use editing tools. This lets you fix videos.**

➡ **Use microphones. Improve the audio quality. Audio is sound. Make sure viewers can hear everything. Viewers watch videos.**

See if you can borrow equipment from your school or library.

Decide the content of the channel. There are different types. These are some examples:

➡ **Be funny. Comedy shows make people laugh.**

➡ **Teach viewers how to do things. These are called guru videos. A guru is an expert.**

➡ **Make music. Share music videos.**

➡ **Share your opinions. Judge the quality of things. Write reviews.**

➡ **Talk about issues. Talk shows are popular. People talk about their favorite topics. They share their thoughts.**

Decide the theme. Themes are main ideas. They're topics.

➡ **Focus on your interests.**

➡ **Focus on what you know.**

➡ **Focus on what you love.**

Show off your strengths.

TRY THIS!

Create an A-to-Z series on your YouTube channel. Go deeper on a topic. Your channel should add value to your viewers' lives. Teach them something. Have them feel happiness. Entertain them.

You'll need: YouTube channel account, computer, Internet, videos

Steps

1 Think of an interesting topic.

2 Explore that topic from A to Z. Create 26 ten-minute videos. Each video should focus on a specific letter.

3 Interview people. Take field trips. Film different things.

4 Move on to a different topic.

Make sure you have good videos.

➡ **Tell a story. Include a beginning. Include a middle. Include an end.**

➡ **Keep videos short. Shorter videos get more views. Stay under 10 minutes. Break up long videos. Make content easy for viewers.**

➡ **Do several takes. A take is a recording.**

➡ **Record more than you need. Edit to fix mistakes.**

➡ **Film in good light. Film during the day. Turn on lots of light.**

➡ **Film good angles. Figure out your best side.**

➡ **Speak loudly. Speak clearly. Voices should be louder than music.**

➡ **Follow YouTube's rules.**

Focus on personal stories.

CHAPTER THREE

HOW DO YOU SET UP A YOUTUBE CHANNEL?

Name the channel.

➡ Connect it to the theme. Relate it to content.

➡ Make the name catchy. You want viewers to remember it.

➡ Be thoughtful about the name. You can't change it.

➡ Be different from other channels. Check if the name is already taken.

CORY DEMEYERS AND JESSE LA FLAIR

Parkour is an extreme sport. It's when people run around and over obstacles. Obstacles are objects in people's paths. They run as fast as possible. YouTube made parkour popular. Cory DeMeyers and Jesse La Flair used YouTube. They have a series on the Web. It's called *Off the Edge*. DeMeyers said, "It is crazy to think that parkour and freerunning are some of the most viewed videos on social media and have been for years, much more than any other sports." La Flair said, "We see in pictures. We're very visual people who grew up in a visual medium." He has several thousand followers. His YouTube channel is the world's most popular parkour channel. They advise posting videos that show moves, experiments, and mistakes. People learn from YouTube. People get inspired by YouTube.

Be excited about your topic.

Describe the channel.

➡ **Let viewers know about your content. Describe the theme.**

➡ **Include fun messages. Entice viewers to watch.**

➡ **Link to other Web sites.**

➡ **Update news. Keep current.**

➡ **Provide basic information. Describe yourself.**

Make sure art is the correct size.

Add channel art. This is an image. It's at the top of the channel page.

➡ Use exciting art. Draw viewers' attention. Make it stand out from the rest of the page. Use friends who have art skills.

➡ Include the channel's name in channel art.

➡ Change channel art. Do this often. Keep the channel fresh. Keep viewers interested.

Create a channel trailer. Trailers are previews. They're videos. They attract viewers. They're like commercials.

➡ Make trailers exciting. Grab viewers' attention in the first few seconds.

➡ Show bits of videos. Show the best parts. These are called teasers. Get viewers interested.

Promote engagement. Engagement is getting lots of people involved.

Design the channel.

→ **Create a home page. Viewers see this page first. This page tracks activities.**

→ **Create playlists. Playlists are lists. They're video collections. Anybody can make playlists. Anybody can share them.**

→ **Start and create discussions. Discussions show comments. Viewers can leave notes. They discuss the videos.**

→ **Add videos. List your videos. List the videos you liked.**

Allow activities on the channel. Encourage viewers to be active.

→ **"Like" videos.**

→ **Comment on videos.**

→ **"Favorite" videos. Viewers can save videos. Favorites are on a special list.**

→ **Subscribe to channels. Viewers can follow your channel.**

Upload videos.

➡ **Click the videos tab. Start uploading.**

➡ **Provide basic information. Add the title. Describe the video topic.**

➡ **Control who watches videos. Click the privacy menu. Send private invitations.**

➡ **Publish the videos. This means the public can see your videos.**

Create video introductions.

➡ **Keep introductions short.**

➡ **Describe what viewers can expect. Don't give away too much information.**

➡ **State the purpose.**

➡ **Show off your personality. Talk directly to viewers. Tell them to watch your channel.**

Keep viewers watching. The longer they watch, the higher your rankings.

CHAPTER FOUR

HOW DO YOU MAINTAIN A YOUTUBE CHANNEL?

You've got videos. You've got a YouTube channel. Now, you need to keep viewers.

Tag videos. Tagging is like sorting. Assign keywords. This makes videos easy to search.

➡ Make tags apply to videos. Tags need to make sense.

➡ Use different tags. Add specific tags. Add broad tags.

➡ Apply several tags. This increases chances of videos being searched.

➡ Create a unique tag. This groups videos together.

Update channel every week.

➡ **Keep uploading videos. Film as much as possible. Keep a steady stream of content.**

➡ **Let viewers know if you're taking breaks. Let them know when you're returning.**

Think about how television shows work. Viewers want new shows each week.

QUICK TIPS

- Include cute pets in your videos. Dogs and cats are a big hit.

- Lock videos. Only people with the Web address can view it. This keeps your privacy.

- Don't be afraid to be weird. People like crazy. Don't be afraid to make mistakes. People like imperfections. These things get attention.

- Stay away from mirrors in your videos. They may add content you don't want.

- Don't let negative comments bother you. Learn from feedback. Keep the comments. Each comment puts the clip on YouTube's "most discussed" list. This means the video is featured in a special section. This can increase viewers.

- Make money on YouTube when you turn 18. This is the legal age. Then, you can create an AdSense account. To make money, you need millions of views.

- Use common sense. Don't break laws. Comply with YouTube's terms. Otherwise, YouTube will remove your video and ban the account.

Interact with viewers. This keeps viewers watching.

⇒ **Respond to comments.**

⇒ **Treat viewers with respect.**

⇒ **Moderate comments. This means you can delete or keep comments.**

⇒ **Pose questions to viewers. Promote good discussions.**

⇒ **Get people to subscribe. This means they'll get automatic updates. Subscribers are your biggest fans.**

⇒ **Continue to put out quality content.**

⇒ **Feature your viewers' videos.**

⇒ **Always thank viewers.**

I Like

LIKE

Increase how many times your channel is viewed.

Spend a lot of time on YouTube.

➡ **Watch other channels.**

➡ **Interact with other users.**

➡ **Search for the same topics.**

➡ **Link to other users' content. This will get your channel to show up on searches.**

Create hype. Hype is excitement.

➡ **Create shorter videos that lead to a longer video. Tell people about upcoming videos. Spread the word.**

➡ **Do live events. Help viewers experience events.**

➡ **Create follow-up videos. Interview viewers about your content.**

Use annotations. These are boxes of text that appear in your video stream. They're like tables of content.

Build a YouTube community.

➡ **Work with other owners. Work with other users.**

➡ **Do guest spots on each other's videos. Invite others to guest speak.**

Promote the channel.

➡ **Use social media.**

➡ **Tell everyone you know.**

➡ **Tell viewers to spread the word.**

➡ **Remind viewers to "like" your videos.**

➡ **Have fun!**

D.I.Y. EXAMPLE!

STEPS	EXAMPLES
Theme	Talk show about retro teen dramas
Description	Throw back and talk about old-school television shows. Go along with Tammy as she power-watches teen drama shows from the 1990s and early 2000s. Laugh at the ridiculousness and wonder if future generations will think our shows are just as goofy.
When	First Saturday of June
Channel name	Teen TV Talk with Tammy
Structure of show	• 10-minute episodes • Open with introduction of Tammy and show • First segment: What just happened?!? (Overview of episode) • Second segment: What's up with that?!? (Commentary on weird things) • Third segment: What else?!? (Commentary on random things) • Special feature: What's hot and what's not?!?

STEPS	EXAMPLES
Film clips	Do talk shows about the retro teen dramas: ♦ *One Tree Hill* ♦ *Dawson's Creek* ♦ *Gossip Girl*
Promotion plan	♦ Share YouTube channel on all my social media sites. ♦ Invite users to chat on the show with me. This will get their viewers to watch as well. ♦ Join online communities around the shows and Netflix.

GLOSSARY

accounts (uh-KOUNTS) usernames and passwords that give people access to a Web site

audio (AW-dee-oh) sound

content (KAHN-tent) videos and comments on one's YouTube channel

fan base (FAN BASE) admirers

guru (GOO-roo) expert

hype (HIPE) excitement

mobile (MOH-buhl) easy to move, portable

moderate (MAH-duh-rate) to check comments and have the ability to delete or add

playlists (PLAY-lists) lists of collected videos

storage (STOR-ij) computer memory, space that holds data

subscribe (suhb-SKRIBE) to follow someone, to get automatic updates

tag (TAG) to catalog, to identify with keywords

takes (TAYKS) recordings

teasers (TEEZ-erz) the best parts of videos shown to entice viewers

theme (THEEM) topic, main idea

trailers (TRAY-lurz) video previews, commercials

users (YOO-zurz) people who use the Internet

viewers (VYOO-urz) people who watch videos

webcam (WEB-kam) camera on a computer

INDEX

LEARN MORE

BOOKS

Ciampa, Rob, Theresa Moore, and John Caruccci. *YouTube Channels for Dummies*. Hoboken, NJ: John Wiley & Sons, 2015.

Cornwall, Phyllis. *Online Etiquette and Safety*. Ann Arbor, MI: Cherry Lake Publishing, 2010.

Woolf, Alex. *Let's Think About the Internet and Social Media*. Chicago: Heinemann-Raintree, 2015.

WEB SITES

WikiHow—How to Make a YouTube Channel: www.wikihow.com/Make-a-YouTube-Channel

WikiHow—How to Make a YouTube Video: www.wikihow.com/Make-a-YouTube-Video